performance!

Peter Biddulph

performance!

musicians in photographs by **clive barda**

For Rozzie

Dame Kiri te Kanawa
Arabella
Royal Opera House
London, 14 July 1977

(previous page)
Sergiu Celibidache
Royal Festival Hall
London, 10 April 1978

ACKNOWLEDGEMENTS

It was Jennifer Laredo who, when looking through some of my photographs, suggested they would make a wonderful book. Her continuing interest, energy, sense of humour and enthusiasm have been a constant inspiration and it is chiefly to her and to Peter Biddulph, without whose unstinting support the project could never have happened, that I owe a huge debt of thanks.

Vladimir Ashkenazy is an artist whose prodigious musical accomplishments are renowned. I have always admired the honesty and integrity of both the man and his art and I am immensely grateful that he agreed to contribute a foreword.

I should also like to thank Colin Ford for agreeing to be my editor and for his wisdom and guidance in the process. In addition to his encyclopaedic knowledge of photography, he has a profound love of music. I have greatly valued the interest he has shown in my work over the years.

Graeme Kay and I have frequently worked together since he mounted an exhibition of my work in Manchester in 1980. His many years at the helm of music and opera magazines give him a great understanding of photography and I am most grateful for his contribution.

I know no better designer than David Pocknell and I was delighted when he agreed to design this book. His colleague Becky Taee has shown fine sensitivity and judgement in working with my pictures and great patience in responding to ideas and suggestions.

Last but by no means least, I want to thank my wife Rozzie for her devotion and unwavering support throughout my career. Words cannot express my gratitude.

Published 2000 by Peter Biddulph,
34 St George Street, London W1S 2ND

Art Direction: David Pocknell
Edited by Colin Ford
Designed by Becky Taee at Pocknell Studio

ISBN 0-9520109-4-1

Originated and printed by Richard Edward Ltd

Vladimir Ashkenazy
All Saints Church
Petersham, 26 March 1977

Foreword

One of the secrets of Clive Barda's continuous success as a highly sought-after photographer of musicians is his rare gift of being unnoticed, discreet and unobtrusive while doing his work. In this respect, he reminds me of the great Ansel Adams, usually renowned for his nature photography. But, proving his versatility, he once took photographs of my wife, moving round her so discreetly that she was barely aware of his presence. The result was probably the most truthful, indeed, the best portrait of my wife that I know.

Clive Barda chose to focus on music, and he too took wonderful pictures of my family when I asked him to a few years ago. The photographs you see in this book speak for themselves, such is the degree of Clive's identification with his subject. Musicians are not the easiest subjects in the world, and it is our good luck that he works with us.

Vladimir Ashkenazy

41

Klaus Tennstedt
Kingsway Hall
London, 4 May 1983

(previous page)
Sir Reginald Goodall
Welsh National Opera,
New Theatre
Cardiff, 13 February 1984

The Music Makers

by **Colin Ford**

'We are the music makers, We are the makers of dreams'. Those words by an obscure Victorian poet only came fully to life – appropriately enough – when set to music by Edward Elgar. Some of the music makers in this book are certainly dreamy and romantic, but most are fiercely energetic, passionate, aggressive, even violent. Music is never static; at its best it is, in every sense of the word, moving.

But photographs are moments frozen in time. I am constantly astonished at the magic ability of a handful of photographers (and even fewer painters) to capture the sense of motion in a still image, not by perceptibly blurring it but by pinpointing the precise point in a movement or gesture when we sense exactly what happened just before that moment, and what will happen immediately after it. Among those special photographers are the American Richard Avedon and the Hungarian André Kertész, who called the moment of exposure the 'culmination – the happening – which I feel coming instinctively'. For the Frenchman Henri Cartier-Bresson it was the 'decisive moment' – the instant when the visual impact and composition of a photograph reflects its precise emotion and meaning. The rare ability to recognise this split second, and to capture it on film, is one of the hallmarks of a fine photographer.

Like those illustrious predecessors, Clive Barda has to be a very precise marksman – and his target is nearly always moving. If architecture is 'music frozen in time', as one nineteenth century art historian called it, Barda's photographs are music frozen on paper. Yet most of them are anything but static.

Carlos Kleiber
Royal Opera House
London, 5 September 1979

This being so, though there are some fine formal portraits in this book, Barda and I found that in making our selection of pictures we often preferred the action shots. There is sufficient material in his library for several books of portraits (each picture in *Performance!* has won its place in competition with hundreds of others with equally compelling claims to be included), but the working shots are always more dynamic, and often more revealing. They show great musicians, not posing or controlling the way they are presented but – at least temporarily – unaware of the camera. Both they and their cameraman are totally caught up in the full flow of the music.

In some ways, it is difficult to understand how anything emotional, cerebral or even aural (such as music) can be portrayed visually. I remember how, when I first began to talk about photographs on radio twenty years ago (initially encouraged by Radio 4's arts programme *Kaleidoscope*), there were those who questioned whether one could possibly communicate anything useful about pictures to an audience which could not see them. But we soon realised that the mind is supremely well equipped to *imagine* pictures, and to flesh out the words we read or hear. Similarly, many who study the following pages will vividly imagine that they can hear the music being performed by these extraordinary women and men. These photographs make true 'music to the eyes'. Clive's own description of what he is trying to do is to grasp 'the feather on the breath of God' – a spontaneous, uncontrolled insight into a performer in action.

Anne Sofie von Otter
La Cenerentola
Royal Opera House
London, 26 June 1991

To watch professional musicians at work is to be in awe of their talent, and of the enormous skill which enables them to vary even tiny details in their performances. In this, at least, there are parallels with photographers. For performer and cameraman alike, the slightest nuance of expression means a great deal; the more closely Barda identifies with the musicians he is photographing the more he finds that their faces and bodies express the music and its mood. Eye contact, body language, and movements of head, arm, hand and finger eloquently convey the sense and emotion of the music. His task is to click the shutter at precisely the right moment. And – in order not to break the spell – he must do so silently!

Portraits have a very different dynamic. For Barda, the rules change completely when someone strikes a pose in front of his camera. When that happens, he must decide whether he believes the pose to be natural – or even honest. Often commissioned by a recording or opera company to make a flattering or attractive likeness, he must also consider if the pose satisfies that brief. At such times, Barda has the words of the great Victorian portraitist Julia Margaret Cameron ringing in his ears: 'When I have such men before my camera my whole soul has endeavoured to do its duty towards them in recording faithfully the greatness of the inner as well as the features of the outer man'. A century and a quarter after this was written, Mrs Cameron's ambition and aspiration are still valid, though today we would add 'women': about a fifth of the pictures in this book are of women (though, interestingly, none is of a composer).

The process by which Clive Barda achieves his extraordinary pictures is, as I have suggested, both special and personal. Perhaps some readers will want to know what contribution his chosen cameras and film make; what lenses bring him so close to the action that we can see the musicians sweat; what exposure times allow such sharp and clear pictures to emerge from frequently gloomy and difficult lighting. I do not have the answers to any of these questions, and I have never asked him. Nor have I ever asked a painter which brushes, paint and palette he uses. A picture must be judged by its ability to move, to excite, to involve: how it does so ultimately remains a mystery. Approach the pictures in *Performance!* in this spirit and I promise you a feast for eye and ear. Here are music makers who can indeed make us dream.

Daniel Barenboim
with London Philharmonic
Orchestra and Edinburgh
Festival Chorus
George Watson College
Edinburgh, 29 August 1972

A Life in Pictures

Interview by **Graeme Kay**

Clive Barda was born in 1945, and spent his early years in Egypt. After the Suez crisis of 1956, his family moved to Britain. While studying for a modern languages degree and working as a commodities broker, Barda developed strong interests in music and photography and these came together with an opportunity to photograph the Israeli pianist and conductor, Daniel Barenboim. This in turn brought an introduction to EMI Records. Barda soon became established as one of the most sought-after documentary and portrait photographers in the classical music world and his work appeared in magazines, newspapers, books and theatre programmes, on posters, records, cassettes and CD sleeves.

In the course of his career, Barda has amassed a collection of around 750,000 photographs of performers, especially musicians; a substantial proportion are of drama, dance, musicals and opera. He has been closely associated with the work of the Royal Opera House, English National Opera, Welsh National Opera, Glyndebourne Festival Opera and Opera North. Among his most notable commissions in musical theatre was photographing the London and New York premières of Andrew Lloyd Webber's immensely popular *Phantom of the Opera*. A major development in Barda's career was the founding in 1990 of Performing Arts Library, both as a showcase for his own collection and an opportunity to present the work of other top photographers working in the arts. PAL is now one of the most comprehensive and technically advanced specialist photo-libraries in the world.

Clive Barda's work has been recognised with exhibitions in Australia, Japan and Britain – in Bradford (National Museum of Photography, Film & Television), Bath (Royal Photographic Society), London and Manchester. He lives in Hammersmith, West London, with his wife Rosalind. They have three sons – Henry, George and Charlie.

BEGINNINGS

Clive Barda never planned a career as a professional photographer of musicians. His original intention was to deepen his knowledge of languages with a degree course at London University and then make a living as a City businessman. Documentary photography was merely a hobby. But a chance occurrence in his early twenties opened up a new interest – classical music. This quickly became a passion, and photography and music were to combine in a new career, kick-started by the traditional 'big break'.

Daniel Barenboim
No 1 Studio,
Abbey Road
London, 22 May 1969

(previous page)
Itzhak Perlman & Pinchas Zukerman
Royal College of Music
London, 24 October 1976

CB: "The first proper concert I ever went to was an evening of Viennese music conducted by Sir John Barbirolli. I was about twenty. Before that, my contact with music had been the usual business of taking piano lessons as a child, being reluctant to practise and finally giving up. The Barbirolli concert was suggested by a flatmate and we went together. It was almost like the conversion on the road to Damascus. I enjoyed the concert so much that I was soon attending several concerts a week and listening regularly to Radio 3, trying to absorb as much as possible about classical music. But when I went to concerts, to be honest, I left all thoughts of photography in the cloakroom with my coat and hat.

Until that point, my interest in photography had been mostly documentary – I was doing photography while studying for my language degree and I combined the two by travelling. On one trip I went to Romania to photograph the painted monasteries of Moldavia. By the time I finished my degree in 1968, I knew I wanted to be a professional photographer. Classical music had become a very important part of my life and, when my 'big break' came along, I was able to combine the two.

Susan Drake
At home
London, 12 November 1968

After completing my degree, I went on holiday to a friend's villa in southern Spain, where I met a journalist working for South Wales Magazine. She advised me to get in touch with the editor and the result was a commission to photograph the harpist Susan Drake. At the time, Susan was married to the brilliant trumpeter John Wilbraham, just launching his solo career with a recording of the Haydn and Hummel trumpet concertos. As he needed photographs, I took some. When the record producer, Mike Bremner, saw the results, he asked me to do the LP sleeve. Susan showed my pictures to her agent, who recommended me to other artists, and my career was launched.

I was starting to get regular commissions and enjoyed working with musicians. In 1969, I went to a concert at London's South Bank, where the pianist Daniel Barenboim and the cellist Jacqueline du Pré were playing Beethoven sonatas. They were the 'golden couple', and Barenboim in particular was flavour-of-the-month. He was the most famous musician I had come close to and I decided to ask if I could photograph him. I waited at the stage door, more-or-less tugged at his sleeve and asked him. To my amazement, Barenboim just said 'OK' and started to move away. 'But when?' He paused: 'Come next Tuesday'. Further slight consternation: 'Mr Barenboim – where?' 'Queen Elizabeth Hall'. On the appointed day I turned up at QEH, where the violinist Pinchas Zukerman was soloist in a concert with Barenboim. I took my photographs and, as this was in the middle of a cycle of South Bank concerts, rushed back to the Royal Festival Hall a couple of days later with my pictures of Barenboim. In the Green Room I met Peter Andry, a senior executive at EMI Records. He suggested that I show them to the art department at EMI, and the immediate result was my first major commission: to photograph Yehudi Menuhin. Within a short time, I had a lot of work lined up with EMI and other record labels."

RECORDING – THE BOOM YEARS

In the 1970s Clive Barda's career as a professional photographer of musicians burgeoned. It was a time of unprecedented growth in the recording industry, fuelled by developments in technology and the determination of such creative artists as the conductor Georg Solti and Decca's John Culshaw (producer of the 'sonic stage' recording of Wagner's *Ring* cycle) to exploit those developments to the full. The stereo hi-fi revolution had made superb sound quality increasingly available to consumers. The full, rich sound and technically flawless playing of the world's great symphony orchestras was available to all at the touch of a button; entire operas could be squeezed on to

Radu Lupu
Winchester College
Winchester, 5 October 1997

no more than two or three LPs and chamber music brought into the home with vivid presence.

Global markets and faster international communications also meant that artists could rapidly become stars in several territories. Record companies considered it artistically essential to make recordings under the most propitious circumstances: the perfect medium required perfect performances. Consequently, rehearsal and recording times were generous and studio preferred to 'live' recording; several days might be allotted for chamber, choral, symphonic and song recordings, entire weeks for opera. To finance all this, companies took the long view (thousands of classic recordings of this period remain cherished in the catalogue today) or justified an element of cross-subsidy for classical music from more popular recorded genres.

Lengthy schedules, and the dominance of the 12-inch Long Playing record, meant that photographers were able to work on a big canvas. In addition to record sleeve photography, detailed booklets for opera recordings demanded lavish photographic illustration, and it was not uncommon for a photographer to be engaged to attend most of the sessions for a recording project. Born into the growing tradition of more relaxed portraiture which influenced both studio and location photography, Clive Barda soon made the style uniquely his own. His approach gives an insight into character by observing both the dramatically expressive gestures used by conductors, singers and instrumentalists and the more intimate moments of relaxation and companionship shared by all musicians in rehearsal and performance.

CB: "The beginning of my career coincided with a time when musicians like Barenboim, Zukerman, Perlman, Kyung-Wha Chung, Radu Lupu and Murray Perahia were beginning to make big names for themselves and good photographs were needed to help promote their careers. What I offered was enthusiasm and close identification with the music. My knowledge was growing along with my workload and, because I spent so many hours with the players, they learned to relax in my presence. They recognised my genuine commitment to their work.

In addition to big LP boxes and booklets, advances in printing technology had created a boom in colour reproduction for newspaper supplements, led in the mass-market by the *Sunday Times* and *Observer*. These supplements were sophisticated outlets for photography and helped to define and shape people's

tastes in photography: think of the war photography of Don McCullin, for instance. Musicians may have been on the periphery of the supplements' interests, but these were great times for photo-reportage of all kinds.

While there were new opportunities for photography, the circumstances under which we had to work were not always ideal. Extended studio sessions and concert rehearsals were one thing, but one had always to remember that the photographer was a guest, a fly-on-the-wall reporter who had to exercise discretion. With more controlled portraiture, some of the expectations of the artists and commissioners could be extremely challenging, not to say frustrating: 'You've got ten minutes in so-and-so's hotel room'; 'you have five minutes between sessions – do what you can'. The notion that an art director could call on a half or even whole day of an artist's time for photography was seldom contemplated.

The tradition of photographing musicians which I inherited was of formal portraits by people like the Fayers (in Vienna) and Lotte Meitner-Graf (in London). Meitner-Graf's famous chiaroscuro 'studies' of musicians offered unprecedented insights into their characters, but were of course static. But Eric Auerbach had shown what could be done in his well-known picture of Ralph Vaughan Williams in old age. The composer is seated, wearing a thick wool suit; his glasses are perched on his forehead, and you can glimpse a hearing aid in his left ear and the battery wire disappearing into his waistcoat; clamped to his right ear is a modern version of an ear trumpet. The picture conveys the vulnerability of an old man suffering the affliction perhaps most feared by composers, deafness. Yet it is in no way exploitative. What shines through is dignity, intelligence and inner strength. Auerbach had seized the moment and produced an image which meant very much more than the sum of its parts.

This style of photography was increasingly typical of what I wanted to do, and fitted in with my interest in reportage. This was facilitated by the long hours of recording sessions. The entire mind-set was different, allowing decisions to be taken primarily for artistic rather than commercial reasons (though a good artistic decision sometimes works out well commercially in the long run). When recording, the red light wouldn't go on until a satisfactory performance had already been worked up in rehearsal. Nowadays, virtually everything which happens throughout the sessions is recorded and much of what you hear on disc is the result of extended digital editing. This change in approach has had a direct impact on my work because, when I am in the studio, although my cameras are the quietest available, I simply must not make any noise when the red light is on.

During those earlier, apparently charmed, years my work had a range and depth which is harder to capture today, if not impossible. Everybody was preoccupied with the need to get recordings right and the aspiration to perfection was paramount; nothing was rushed or skimped. The fact that I often spent hours with the artists and was perceived to be a member of the recording team fed into my work in a number of ways: repeated encounters in the studio and canteen bolstered my sense of affinity with the musicians and their work. The generous recording schedules even allowed for a modicum of 'fooling around', helping everyone to relax and defusing some of the tensions which inevitably arise from time to time."

PASSIONATE ENGAGEMENT

Over the years, Clive Barda has worked with all of the world's major classical musicians. He began his career as some entered the twilight of theirs; he has followed others through their entire creative lives; there are always new talents to encounter and engage with. But the explosion in printed, recorded and broadcast media of the last three decades, of which photography is an important part, has given him a vital role in the long-term perception of classical music. Much of his work depends on striking a balance between documentary reportage and a level of personal involvement and commitment which few other photographers have achieved.

CB: "The importance of the media in our society means that my work has played a part in the way creative artists are portrayed. Musicians combine their creative energies as interpreters with those of the composer. It's a process of discovery which is never ending and never static. In performance, musicians are constantly summoning up great reserves of passion and power and battling with the frustrations of not getting the right result. When recording, they can't allow chance to play the same role. If something isn't going well, they may explode in temper or frustration and I must make an instant judgment as to whether or not to photograph this lapse of control, which might be an abuse of the confidence placed in me. On the other hand, the urge to document and produce a rounded overall portrait may influence my decision. I think it's right that the humanity and vulnerability of artists should be shown, as well as their obvious strengths and triumphs, but I would never want my presence to inflame a situation. If I'm working on commission, however, pictures

Maurice André
No 1 Studio,
Abbey Road
London,
24 January 1977

considered inappropriate would never be used for promotion, but may have an extended life as historical documents.

These decisions require professional detachment. There have been times when I have been moved to tears – not the best state to be in when taking pictures. Although the benefits of being so closely connected with what is going on are self-evident, there is a danger of being distracted if you allow yourself to get carried away. One such occasion I remember was when I was a member of the audience at a concert by the young cellist Adrian Brendel. He and two young colleagues were playing Beethoven's *Archduke Trio*, which I know well and love. I suddenly found myself so detached from reality that I was almost under the impression it was I playing the cello: I felt I knew exactly what was going to happen next in the music, because I was in control of it. It was almost an out-of-body experience. I am convinced that music is transcendental – that it can take possession of you. At these times I enjoy a rather strange, almost mystical identification with the music.

Opera exemplifies this, deriving from the voice, the human organ itself. All instruments seek to emulate the voice in some way. The whole experience of opera, and the events and emotions played out on stage, speak directly to the spectator's heart. One piece which almost invariably brings tears to my eyes is Wotan's Farewell from Act 3 of Wagner's *Die Walküre*. At that overwhelming moment in the score, Wagner seems to have arrived at a combination of sounds which tap into the human pulse and override one's intellectual control mechanisms. It's like being tripped over. I've been to performances of Wagner where hardened businessmen have come into the theatre after a stressful day at the office and have ended up sobbing quietly into their hankies. I remember an occasion when the American mezzo-soprano Jane Henschel took part in a charity concert for the Children of the Andes. She sang Eboli's aria, 'O don fatale' from Verdi's *Don Carlos* – not music that I had any particular connection with. It really hit me, like being punched in the solar plexus.

All these experiences have led me to think about the nature of greatness in musicians. I think it's an essential precondition of greatness in a performance that one is more aware of the music than of the musician. But my job as a photographer is to concentrate on the performer. If you're really plugged into the music you begin to understand – often through scarcely perceptible shifts in position of the hands, the angle of the body, or a facial expression – that an interpretation is reflected in each individual performer's vocabulary of

Valery Gergiev
Philharmonic Hall
Rotterdam
27-28 November 1997

(following page, left)
Vladimir Horowitz
Royal Festival Hall
London, 18 May 1982

(following page, right)
Evgeny Kissin
Barbican Concert Hall
London, 6 June 1996

movements. When these instants come, it helps to be immersed in the music – often though I can't tell if I've captured them until I see the contact sheets.

Over time, I have become familiar with the repertoire, but today's performers range much further afield than the musicians of thirty years ago. From a photographic point of view, I can anticipate a certain amount with a general 'feel' for musical idiom and knowing how a passage is likely to develop. But in contemporary music there is no predictable pattern: if the music is wildly extrovert, I can capture amazing variety of expression. In purely practical terms, there is the added disadvantage that conductors tend to have their heads down most of the time, following the score intently. Fortunately, however, the kind of big scores you get in this music tend to reflect lots of light into their faces!

I am often asked how the great artists of today compare with giants of previous generations. My response is that one is not comparing apples with apples. Today's performers certainly have the requisite technique. But the infrastructure which creates and nurtures them is quite different. They have grown up with popular music being pumped at them unbidden from every direction. Recordings of the standard repertoire by other artists form a large part of their musical education. Even the social environment is different – artists are expected to be accessible and telegenic. Yet only a small part of their potential public is able to make an informed assessment of how they fit into the continuum of performance history.

If performers are lucky enough to be invited to make recordings, they will find an entirely changed business. In the case of big projects such as operas and symphonies, 'live' recordings have taken precedence over the studio for economic reasons. Marketing considerations rather than artistic ones define the approach to the way their images are projected. If an art director decides that biker leathers will grace the front cover of the CD, this will happen, even if the musician in question has never climbed on a motorbike in his or her entire life. In this way, marketing people seek to control the central image and thus maximise the 'asset value' of the musician. I find this a rather heartless approach to gifted people, and my personal knowledge of the artists tells me that the images chosen to market their talents often contradict their personalities. In my own work I always strive to present something more truthful."

SONS

Rudolf Serkin
Kingsway Hall
London, 6 September 1981

(opposite page)
Mstislav Rostropovich
No 1 Studio, Abbey Road
London, 20 April 1978

(previous page)
Evgeny Kissin
Barbican Concert hall
London, 6 June 1996

Anne-Sophie Mutter
Royal Festival Hall
London, 18 February 1988

(opposite page)
Mirella Freni
as *Madame Butterfly*
Chalk Farm Studios
London,
12 February 1988

(previous page, left)
Daniil Shafran
Wigmore Hall
London, 24 April 1995

(previous page, right)
Jacqueline du Pré
The Fairfield Halls
Croydon
30 January 1970

Lucia Popp
St. John's, Smith Square
London, 23 August 1985

(opposite page)
Roberto Alagna &
Angela Gheorghiu
La Traviata
Royal Opera House
London, 6 July 1996

(previous page)
Agnes Baltsa
Carmen
Royal Opera House
London, 15 May 1986

Teresa Stratas
Covent Garden
London, 17 July 1979

(opposite page)
Amanda Roocroft
Glyndebourne, 14 July 1994

Oliver Knussen &
Peter Serkin
Henry Wood Hall
London, 14 December 1997

(both pictures)
Alfred Brendel
Usher Hall
Edinburgh, 24 August 1997

Artur Rubinstein
Bishopsgate Hall
London, 2-6 October 1973

Artur Rubinstein
Kingsway Hall
London, 10 March 1975

How things have changed! I was commissioned by RCA Records to photograph the great Polish virtuoso Artur Rubinstein. He always took a suite at the Savoy and, when I arrived at the hotel's reception desk, I was asked to go straight up to his room. I was surprised when the octogenarian maestro opened the door to me himself. He was charm personified. 'Thank you so much for coming,' was his rather disarming greeting to someone who was paid to be there: 'I've spent an hour putting my hair up for you'. 'Maestro, you shouldn't have gone to all that trouble on my account'. 'No, no... you see, I am bald!' It was a complete revelation that what I had always taken to be a full, if eccentrically coiffed, head of hair was in fact a very long skein – woven together likes a bird's nest and held in place with hair lacquer. I was both shocked and humbled to be entrusted with such a peculiar intimacy from a man I had so long admired but never met.

Hair lacquer made another appearance when I went to photograph Rubinstein recording a Beethoven piano concerto. I was amazed to see him spray the piano keys with a can of hair spray before sitting down to play. 'At my age, my skin is papery', he confided, 'and I need extra purchase on the keys'. I still have the can, and have since been told by Steinway's piano technician that Elnet is only one of many such substances which pianists inflict on pianos in the interests of extra adhesion.

Ravi Shankar
Barbican Concert Hall
London, 18 March 1997

John Williams
CBS Studios, Whitfield Street
London, 28 February 1974

Sir Geraint Evans
Die Meistersinger
von Nürnberg
London Opera Centre
London, 6 June 1978

(opposite page)
Sir Thomas Allen
Die Meistersinger
von Nürnberg
Royal Opera House
London, 13 May 2000

Bernard Haitink
Royal Opera House
London, 11 October
2000

Pierre Boulez
Barbican Concert Hall
London, 14 January 1989

(opposite page)
Antonio Pappano
Usher Hall
Edinburgh, 28 August 1997

(opposite page)
Aaron Copland
No 1 Studio,
Abbey Road
London, c1971

(left)
Sir Harrison Birtwistle
Berlin, 23 March 2000

(right)
Pierre Boulez
Barbican Concert Hall
London, 1 February 2000

Hans Werner Henze
Henry Wood Hall
London, 13 June 1996

(opposite page)
Aram Khachaturian
No 1 Studio,
Abbey Road
London, 2 February 1977

Karlheinz Stockhausen
No 1 Studio,
Abbey Road
London, 20 March 1973

(opposite page)
György Kurtág
Queen's Hall
Edinburgh, 25 August 1999

Olivier Messiaen
At the Festival
Bath, 27 May 1986

(opposite page)
Sir Malcolm Arnold
Walthamstow Town Hall
London, 28 October 1986

Philip Glass
At home
New York, 26 February 1985

György Ligeti
Westbury Hotel
London, 21 May 1982

Toru Takemitsu
At the Festival
Aldeburgh, 13 June 1993

(opposite page)
Mark-Anthony Turnage
At home
London, 8 June 1988

Sir Richard Rodney Bennett
Queen Elizabeth Hall
London, 28 May 1986

(opposite page)
Luciano Berio
BBC Maida Vale Studios
London, 17 August 1974

Arvo Pärt
St Marylebone Church
London, 27 March 2000

Sir Peter Maxwell Davies
Clive Barda's Studio
London, 12 August 1974

(opposite page)
Stephen Sondheim
CBS Studios, Whitfield Street
London, 15 May 1976

Witold Lutoslawski
Queen Elizabeth Hall
London, 5 December 1985

John Ogdon
Fairfield Halls
Croydon, c1972

When John Ogdon was at the height of his fame, having been the first British pianist ever to win the Moscow Tchaikovsky Competition, my wife and I were invited to spend quite a lot of time, socially and professionally, with him and his wife Brenda Lucas. Their insistence that I photograph the major events in John's brilliant career spilled over into private life – a slightly uncomfortable situation for me. For all the incidental pleasures of, for example, having a box at the Royal Albert Hall at the Last Night of the Proms, and being ferried to and from home and the post-concert dinner in a white Rolls-Royce, I felt that the highly pressurised social side of John's life was somehow at odds with the intense nature of his musical gift. This perception seemed to be confirmed by the tragic onset of mental illness, and his subsequent death. I sensed that John was somehow a victim of his own genius. For me, it was a keen if thoroughly unwelcome insight into the degree of personal danger which can attach to any great gift.

Stephen Kovacevich
Barbican Concert Hall
London, 16 February 1986

(opposite page)
Claudio Arrau
Royal Albert Hall
London, 6 June 1976

(previous page)
Murray Perahia
CBS Studios,
Whitfield Street
London, 30 May 1973

András Schiff
Queen's Hall
Edinburgh, 25 August 2000

(opposite page)
Maurizio Pollini
Royal Festival Hall
London, 28 April 1997

Mitsuko Uchida
Royal Festival Hall
London, 12 December 1991

Emil Gilels
No 1 Studio,
Abbey Road
London c1972

(opposite page)
Sir Clifford Curzon
Palais des Congrès
Paris, 21-22 October 1975

MUSIC
INTERNATIONAL MUSIC COMPANY

Carlo Bergonzi
Clive Barda's Studio
London, 21 March 1978

(opposite page)
Yehudi Menuhin
(Lord Menuhin)
No 1 Studio,
Abbey Road
London, 1969

I've paired these two artists not because they ever performed together but because I had a similar experience with each of them. Menuhin had been one of my earliest commissions from EMI, and over the years I grew to know him and many members of his family extremely well. On one memorable occasion I went to meet him at the home of his son Jeremy and Menuhin absolutely insisted on helping me carry my rather heavy lights up the stairs to the flat. I was concerned about damage to his hands, but he would have none of it.

Another time, I was asked to photograph Menuhin with the pianist Louis Kentner in connection with a TV documentary. The filming took place at Kentner's house in Chelsea. After everything was set up, the film people went off for a break. Menuhin and Kentner decided to rehearse Beethoven's Spring Sonata and I found myself – incredibly – enjoying a private performance by arguably one of the greatest violinists there has ever been.

I felt privileged and humble, as I did when I was asked to photograph Carlo Bergonzi – one of the last great Italian tenors of the old school – at the Royal Opera House. He had arrived to take over in the middle of a run of Donizetti's *L'Elisir d'Amore* and I was invited to attend the orchestral rehearsal. On stage were Bergonzi, in the pit the orchestra and conductor, in the 1800-seat auditorium just me. I feared I would not get precisely the photographs I was looking for, because Bergonzi would just 'mark' the performance, i.e. sing the notes, or most of them, in a voice-conserving whisper. To my amazement, he used his full voice throughout – especially in 'Una furtiva lagrima' – as if his life depended on it. I felt rather like those European kings and princelings who could command a performance for their exclusive pleasure merely by snapping their fingers.

Gidon Kremer
St John's, Smith Square
London, 2 February 1980

(opposite page)
Nathan Milstein
Royal Festival Hall
London, 25 March 1979

Igor Oistrakh
Henry Wood Hall
London, 4 March 1991

Kyung-Wha Chung
BBC Studio,
Broadcasting House
London, 1969

(opposite page)
Ida Haendel
Royal Albert Hall
London, 30 June 1976

Viktoria Mullova
Barbican Concert Hall
London, 21 April 1994

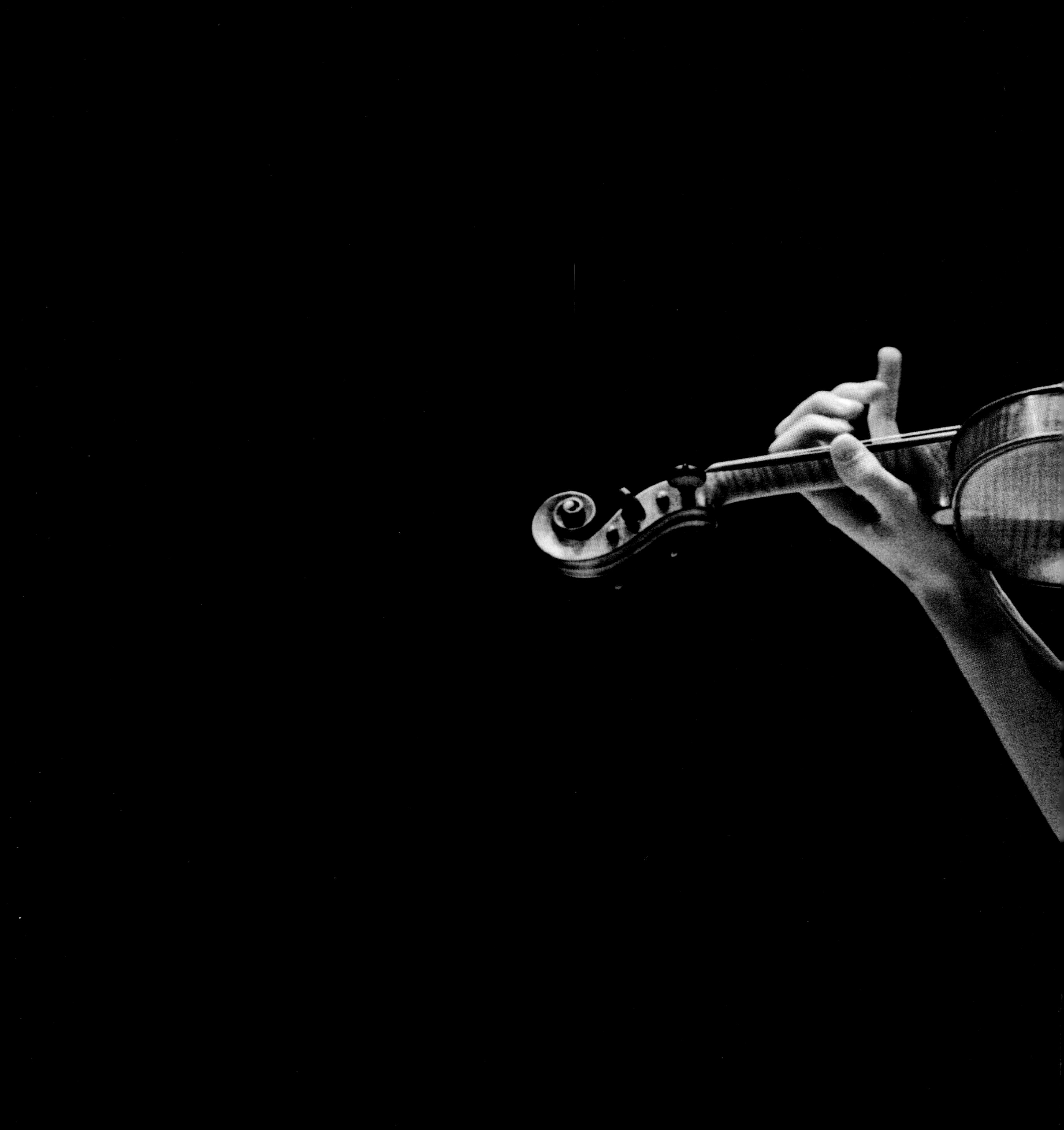

Isaac Stern
Royal Festival Hall
London, 11 February 1979

(opposite page)
Thomas Zehetmair
Usher Hall
Edinburgh, 17 August 1998

Riccardo Chailly
Barbican Concert Hall
London, 24 April 1994

(opposite page)
Daniele Gatti
Barbican Concert Hall
London, 25 May 1995

Maxim Shostakovich
Barbican Concert Hall
London, 7 March 1991

(following page, left)
Rafael Kubelik
Royal Festival Hall
London, 1 July 1980

(following page, right)
Yuri Temirkanov
Royal Festival Hall
London, 13 February 1991

Carlo Maria Giulini
Henry Wood Hall
London, 6 March 1986

(previous page, left)
Leopold Stokowski
West Ham
London, 24 May 1976

(previous page, right)
Eugene Ormandy
Royal Festival Hall
London, 7 May 1975

Zubin Mehta
Barbican Concert Hall
London, 18 March 1997

(following page)
Sir Adrian Boult
Royal Albert Hall
London, 16 October 1976

Bath Festival
30 May-1 June 1995

(top left)
Joshua Bell

(top right)
Pamela Frank

(bottom left)
Jon Kimura Parker

(bottom right)
Tabea Zimmermann

(opposite page)
Steven Isserlis

(left to right)
Pamela Frank, Joshua Bell, Jon Kimura Parker, Tabea Zimmermann, Steven Isserlis
Bath Festival
30 May-1 June 1995

'The musicians I work with are different from normal people. They have a gift which compels them to spend hours and hours every day of their lives trying to develop, refine and perfect their art. Most people can't comprehend such a commitment.'

YoYo Ma
Teatro Communale
Florence, 21 June 1993

Yan Pascal Tortelier
Henry Wood Hall
London, 23 September 1984

(opposite page)
Paul Tortelier
No 1 Studio,
Abbey Road
London,
16 November 1984

Lionel Tertis
At home
London, 30 November 1973

Yuri Bashmet
Royal Albert Hall
London, 9 August 1996

Evelyn Glennie
Windsor Festival
Windsor, 22 September 1996

((opposite page)
Evelyn Glennie
Eton College
Eton, 28 April 1991

Daniel Barenboim &
Jacqueline du Pré
Outside St Paul's
Cathedral
London, 4 July 1976

'I am constantly looking for the opportunity to capture a shot that will add up to more than the sum of its parts: one that can stand outside its own specific context and move both the music lover and the viewer who knows nothing about music.'

Cecilia Bartoli
Café near
Teatro Comunale
Bologna, 16 June 1992

(opposite page)
José Cura
Walthamstow Town Hall
London, 8 July 1999

(opposite page)
Dame Josephine Barstow
Medea
Opera North
Leeds, 17 April 1996

(left)
Dame Janet Baker
Alceste
Royal Opera House
London, 24 November 1981

(right)
Dame Felicity Lott
Die Rosenkavalier
Royal Opera House
London, 1 February 1995

Ileana Cotrubas
Tales of Hoffman
Royal Opera House
London, 12 December 1980

(opposite page)
Dame Joan Sutherland
Lucia di Lammermoor
Royal Opera House
London, 10 April 1985

CLAUDIO

David Daniels
Theodora
Glyndebourne Festival Opera
Glyndebourne, 11 May 1996

(opposite page)
Claudio Abbado &
Teresa Berganza
Carmen
St John's, Smith Square
London, 15 September 1977

James Levine &
Renata Scotto
No 1 Studio,
Abbey Road
London, 12 August 1977

(opposite page)
James Levine
No 1 Studio,
Abbey Road
London, 12 August 1977

Sir Charles Groves and grandson
At home
London, 1 June 1973

Sir Andrew Davis
No 1 Studio,
Abbey Road
London, 7 September 1996

(opposite page)
Sir Andrew Davis
The Organ Room
Glyndebourne, 6 August 1973

Mark Elder
Royal Albert Hall
London, 23 July 1999

(opposite page)
Paul Daniel
Barbican Concert Hall
London, 29 April 1996

(previous page, left)
Jeffrey Tate
Philharmonie
Berlin, 14-17 August 1987

(previous page, right)
Sir Charles Mackerras
No 1 Studio,
Abbey Road
London, 24 January 1977

Daniel Harding
Barbican Concert Hall
London, 2 May 1996

Sir John Eliot Gardiner
All Saints Church, Tooting
London, 18 March 1986

Sir Georg Solti
Royal Festival Hall
London, 1 May 1995

(previous page, left)
Sir Roger Norrington
Royal Festival Hall
London, 24 November 1999

(previous page, right)
Sir Neville Marriner
CBS Studios, Whitfield St
London, 23 August 1974

In 1984 I was commissioned by the Royal Opera House to photograph their new John Schlesinger production of Richard Strauss's Der Rosenkavalier, with Kiri Te Kanawa as the Marschallin, Agnes Baltsa as Octavian and Barbara Bonney as Sophie. Photography at the ROH serves the dual purpose of publicity and archive and, though a certain amount of preparatory photography can be done in earlier rehearsals, the crucially important occasion is the full dress rehearsal. Things had not been going well, as Agnes Baltsa had refused to wear her costume and no photographs had been possible. The conductor, Georg Solti, had a strong aversion to the presence of cameras at rehearsals and I knew that I would need my quietest cameras and be further back in the auditorium than usual. When I arrived for the dress rehearsal I was met by a departing news photographer with the scarcely credible information that 'We've been sent home – there's no Octavian'. I thought this was a joke in poor taste, but my colleague was right. Miss Baltsa's artistic differences had proved irreconcilable and she had left the previous evening.

As a full house of expectant Friends of Covent Garden waited for the dress rehearsal to begin, the atmosphere crackled with the pent-up energy of an imminent eruption by the volcanic Hungarian maestro. But the British mezzo-soprano Anne Howells was tracked down in a supermarket checkout queue and persuaded to take over as Octavian for the dress rehearsal. As the rehearsal started, the sense of relief was palpable. But for me the nightmare soon began again. Solti, whose hearing was acute enough pick up even my 'silenced' Leica at twenty yards, turned aside and shouted, 'No photographs'. Katharine Wilkinson, the press officer, hissed, 'Carry on!' I complied, only to hear another outburst from Solti. During the interval, discreet advice was sought from Solti's wife, Valerie. 'Georg has a stiff neck,' she said sagely: 'he doesn't like looking to the left'. So I moved to the other side of the auditorium and lowered my tripods so that he couldn't see anything when he entered the pit for Act II. I shot the show and Anne Howells made such a good job of Octavian that she was engaged for the entire run and the subsequent video recording.

Eugen Jochum
No 1 Studio,
Abbey Road
London, 30 June 1978

Plácido Domingo
Parsifal
Kirov Opera
St Petersburg, 25 October 1997

(previous page)
Luciano Pavarotti
L'Elisir d'Amore
Royal Opera House
London, 10 March 1990

(following page)
José Carreras
(with Teresa Berganza)
Carmen
Royal Opera House
London, 16 October 1984

Tatiana Troyanos
& Renata Scotto
Henry Wood Hall
London, 19 July 1979

Ileana Cotrubas
& Teresa Berganza
King's Theatre
Edinburgh, 27 August 1977

Christa Ludwig
Elektra
Staatsoper
Hamburg, 9-11 March 1987

(opposite page)
Grace Bumbry
Salome
Royal Opera House
London, 31 October 1977

John Tomlinson
St John's, Smith Square
London, 12 August 1982

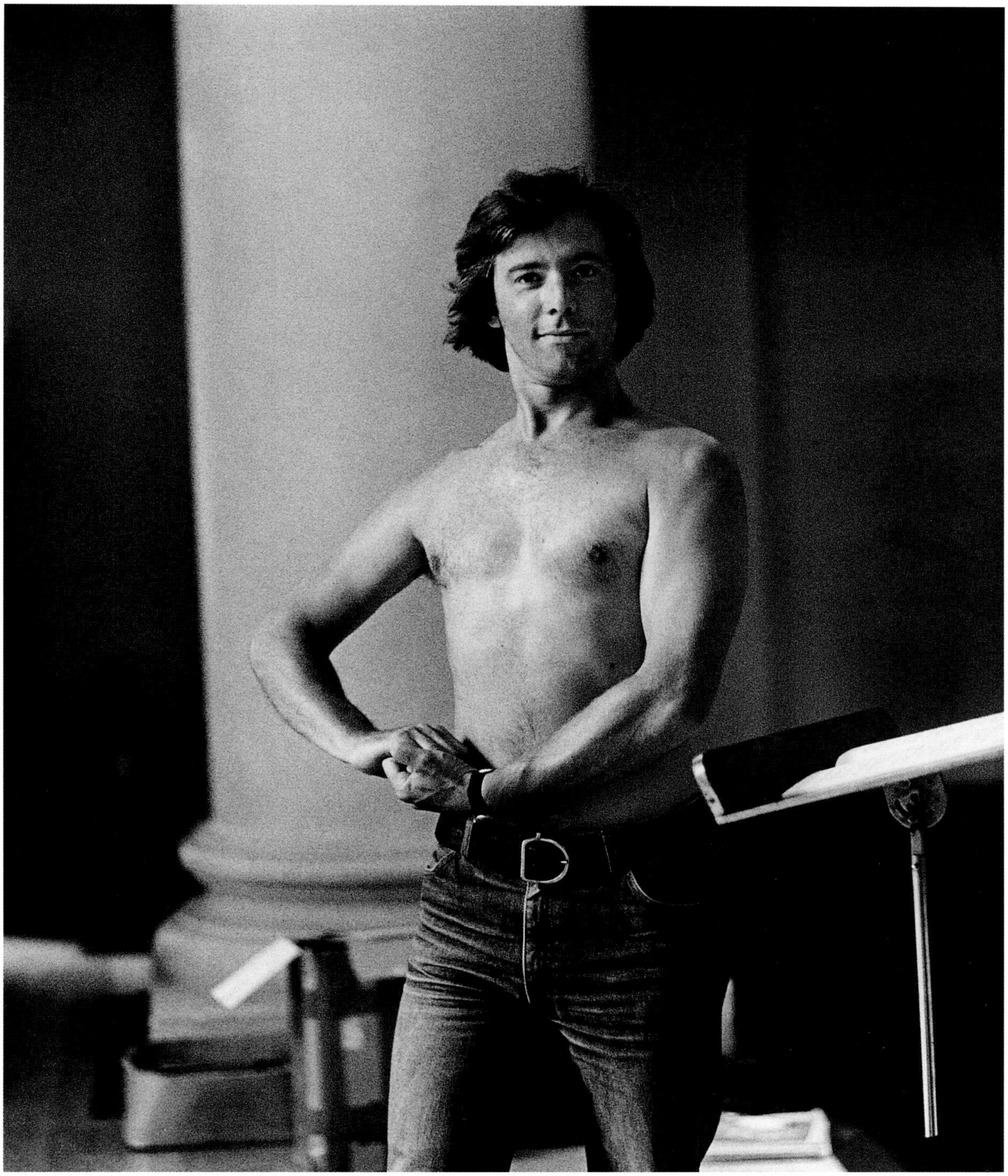

John Tomlinson
Die Meistersinger
von Nürnberg
Royal Opera House
London, 2 October 1993

Radu Lupu
& Murray Perahia
The Maltings, Snape
Suffolk, 26 June 1984

Sviatoslav Richter
Air Studios
London, 22 November 1993

The picture opposite is a fascinating example of the multi-layered meanings a single image can convey. To an English audience at least, the gesture Sviatoslav Richter is making might be interpreted as rude – or at any rate coarse. Clearly this was not his intention, as can be deduced from his weary, resigned expression. In fact, the photo was taken during a rehearsal with Christoph Eschenbach and the English Chamber Orchestra and the pianist was simply indicating which movement he wished to rehearse next. I am amused by the very obvious misinterpretation the photo invites at first glance. But I am confident that, like me, every one who studies it will have second thoughts, and realise what a tortured life this highly sensitive artist led, poignantly conveyed by the tired expression in his eyes and the deeply etched lines in his face. What a wealth of humour, humanity and sadness can be captured in a mere sixtieth of a second!

Sir Peter Pears
Royal Opera House
London, 1 June 1973

(opposite page)
Benjamin Britten
(Lord Britten)
The Maltings, Snape
Suffolk, 11 June 1976

Barry Tuckwell
At home
London, 17 October 1978

Victoria de los Angeles
BBC Studio, Egton House
London, 29 April 1978

(opposite page)
Leontyne Price
Walthamstow Town Hall
London, 31 July 1979

Jessye Norman
Berkeley Square
London, 8 August 1985

David Munrow
No 1 Studio,
Abbey Road
London, c1969

(opposite page)
Jean-Pierre Rampal
Olympic Studios
London, 22 December 1980

Kurt Sanderling
Kingsway Hall
London, 15 January 1981

(opposite page)
Günter Wand
Usher Hall
Edinburgh, 31 August 1999

Vladimir Ashkenazy
Royal Festival Hall
London, 30 November 1999

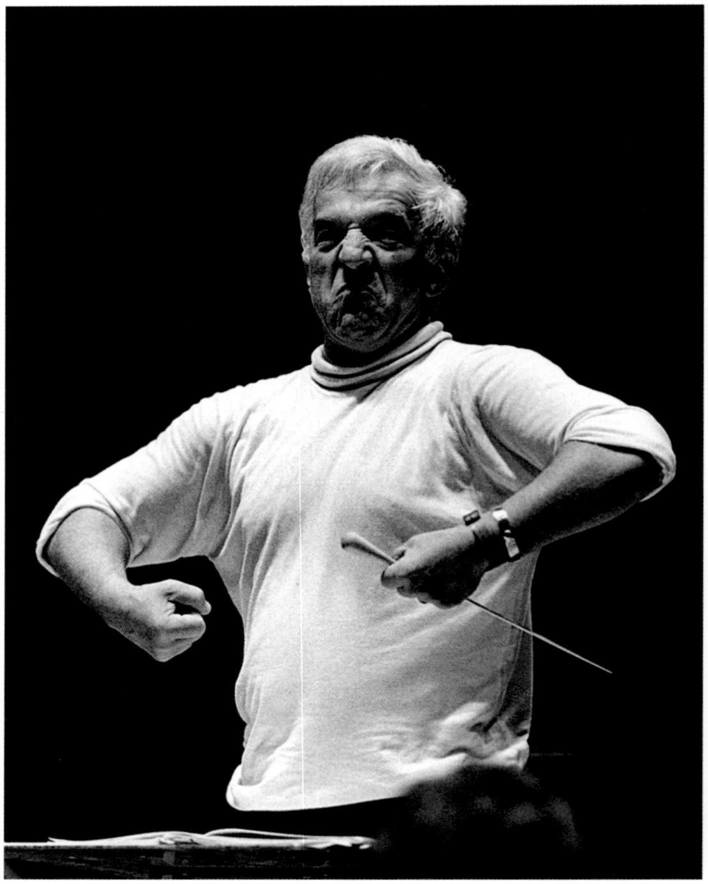

Christian Thielemann
Festspielhaus
Baden-Baden, 5 June 1998

(previous page, left)
Kurt Masur
Barbican Concert Hall
London, 21 April 1994

(previous page, right)
Christoph von Dohnányi
Royal Opera House
London, 7 November 1990

(following page, left)
Leonard Slatkin
Royal Festival Hall
London, 16 March 2000

(following page, right)
Sir Colin Davis
Barbican Concert Hall
London, 16 February 1995

Lorin Maazel
Royal Festival Hall
London, 15 December 1993

(previous page, left)
Michael Tilson Thomas
Barbican Concert Hall
London, 30 September 1990

(previous page, right)
Giuseppe Sinopoli
Royal Festival Hall
London, 15 March 1990

André Previn
Morley College
London, c1971

Leonard Bernstein
Royal Albert Hall
London, 1970-2

Dietrich Fischer-Dieskau
Royal Festival Hall
London, 14 December 1976

(opposite page)
Pierre Fournier
& Mstislav Rostropovich
Royal Festival Hall
London, 11 May 1980

(previous page)
Dame Joan Sutherland
& Luciano Pavarotti
Die Fledermaus
Royal Opera House
London
31 December 1990

An Illustrated Index

Abbado, Claudio
Conductor
Born Milan, Italy 1933
Page 138

Alagna, Roberto
Tenor
Born Paris, France 1964
Page 43

Allen, Sir Thomas
Baritone
Born Seaham Harbour, UK 1944
Page 57

André, Maurice
Trumpeter
Born Alès, France 1933
Page 26

Angeles, Victoria de los
Soprano
Born Barcelona, Spain 1923
Page 171

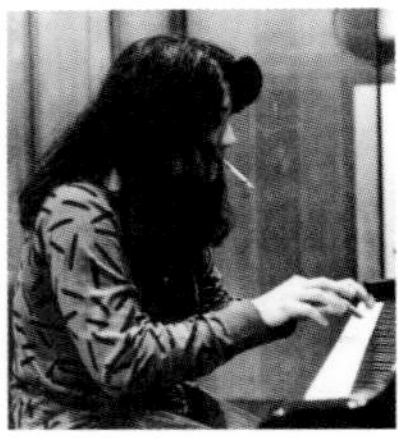

Argerich, Martha
Pianist
Born Buenos Aires, Argentina 1941
Pages 184-5

Arnold, Sir Malcolm
Composer
Born Northampton, UK 1921
Page 68

Arrau, Claudio
Pianist
Born Chillàn, Chile 1903
Died 1991
Page 86

Ashkenazy, Vladimir
Pianist and conductor
Born Nizhniy Novgorod, Russia 1937
Pages 6, 188-9

Baker, Dame Janet
Mezzo-soprano
Born Hatfield (Yorkshire), UK 1933
Page 135

Baltsa, Agnes
Mezzo-soprano
Born Lefkas, Greece 1944
Page 40-1

Barenboim, Daniel
Pianist and conductor
Born Buenos Aires, Argentina 1942
Pages 14-15, 18, 130

Barstow, Dame Josephine
Soprano
Born Yorkshire, UK 1940
Page 134

Bartoli, Cecilia
Mezzo-soprano
Born Rome, Italy 1966
Page 132

Bashmet, Yuri
Viola player
Born Rostoff-on-Don, Russia 1953
Page 127

Bell, Joshua
Violinist
Born Bloomington, USA 1967
Pages 119, 120-1

Bennett, Sir Richard Rodney
Composer
Born Broadstairs, UK 1936
Page 74

Berganza, Teresa (r)
Mezzo-soprano
Born Madrid, Spain 1935
Pages 138,162-3, 165

Bergonzi, Carlo
Tenor
Born Vidalenzo, Italy 1924
Page 95

Berio, Luciano
Composer
Born Oneglia, Italy 1925
Page 75

Bernstein, Leonard
Composer and conductor
Born Lawrence, USA 1918
Died 1990
Page 205

Birtwistle, Sir Harrison
Composer
Born Accrington, UK 1934
Page 63

Boulez, Pierre
Conductor
Born Montbrison, France 1925
Pages 61, 63

Boult, Sir Adrian
Conductor
Born Chester, UK 1889
Died 1983
Pages 116-7

Bream, Julian
Guitarist and lutenist
Born London, UK 1933
Page 54-5

Brendel, Alfred
Pianist
Born Wiesenberg, Germany 1931
Page 48-9

Britten, Lord (Benjamin)
Composer
Born Lowestoft, UK 1913
Died 1976
Page 179

Bumbry, Grace
Mezzo-soprano
Born St Louis, USA 1937
Page 167

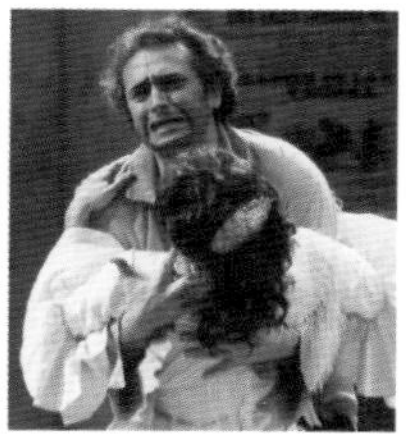

Carreras, José
Tenor
Born Barcelona, Spain 1946
Pages 162-3

Celibidache, Sergiu
Conductor
Born Roman, Romania 1912
Died 1996
Page 2-3

Chailly, Riccardo
Conductor
Born Milan, Italy 1953
Page 107

Chung, Kyung-Wha
Violinist
Born Seoul, South Korea 1948
Page 100

Copland, Aaron
Composer
Born New York, USA 1900
Died 1990
Page 62

Cotrubas, Ileana
Soprano
Born Galati, Romania 1939
Pages 136, 165

Cura, José
Tenor
Born Rosario, Argentina 1962
Page 133

Curzon, Sir Clifford
Pianist
Born London, UK 1907
Died 1982
Page 92

Daniel, Paul
Conductor
Born Birmingham, UK 1958
Page 149

Daniels, David
Countertenor
Born Spartanburg, USA 1966
Page 139

Davis, Sir Andrew
Conductor
Born Ashridge, UK 1944
Pages 144-5

Davis, Sir Colin
Conductor
Born Weybridge, UK 1927
Page 199

Dohnányi, Christoph von
Conductor
Born Berlin, Germany 1929
Page 195

Domingo, Placido
Tenor
Born Madrid, Spain 1941
Pages 160-1

Drake, Susan
Harpist
Born Cardiff, UK 1946
Page 20

du Pré, Jacqueline
Cellist
Born Oxford, UK 1945
Pages 37, 130

Elder, Mark
Conductor
Born Hexham, UK 1947
Pages 148

Evans, Sir Geraint
Baritone
Born Pontypridd, UK 1922
Died 1992
Page 56

Fischer-Dieskau, Dietrich
Baritone
Born Berlin, Germany 1925
Page 208

Fournier, Pierre (I)
Cellist
Born Paris, France 1906
Died 1986
Page 209

Frank, Pamela
Violinist
Born New York, USA 1967
Pages 119, 120-1

Freni, Mirella
Soprano
Born Modena, Italy 1935
Page 39

Gardiner, Sir John Eliot
Conductor
Born Fontmell Magna, UK 1943
Page 151

Gatti, Daniele
Conductor
Born Milan, Italy 1962
Page 106

Gergiev, Valery
Conductor
Born Moscow, Russia 1953
Page 29

Gheorghiu, Angela
Soprano
Born Adjud, Romania 1965
Page 43

Gilels, Emil
Pianist
Born Odessa,
Ukraine 1916
Died 1985
Page 93

Giulini, Carlo Maria
Conductor
Born Berletta, Italy 1914
Page 114

Glass, Philip
Composer
Born Chicago,
USA 1937
Page 70

Glennie, Evelyn
Percussionist
Born Aberdeen,
UK 1965
Pages 128-9

Goodall, Sir Reginald
Conductor
Born Lincoln, UK 1901
Died 1990
Pages 8-9

Grappelli, Stephane (r)
Violinist
Born Paris, France 1908
Died 1997
Back cover

Groves, Sir Charles
Conductor
Born London, UK 1915
Died 1992
Page 142-3

Haendel, Ida
Violinist
Born Chelm,
Poland 1924
Page 101

Haitink, Bernard
Conductor
Born Amsterdam,
Netherlands 1929
Page 58-9

Harding, Daniel
Conductor
Born Cardiff, UK 1975
Page 150

Henze, Hans Werner
Composer
Born Götersloh,
Germany 1926
Page 64

Horowitz, Vladimir
Pianist
Born Kiev, Ukraine 1904
Died 1989
Page 30

Isserlis, Steven
Cellist
Born London, UK 1958
Pages 118, 120-1

Jochum, Eugen
Conductor
Born Babenhausen,
Germany 1902
Died 1989
Pages 156-7

Kanawa, Dame Kiri Te
Soprano
Born Gisborne,
New Zealand 1944
Page 5

Khachaturian, Aram
Composer
Born Tbilisi,
Georgia 1903
Died 1978
Page 65

Kimura Parker, Jon
Pianist
Born Vancouver,
Canada 1959
Pages 119, 120-1

Kissin, Evgeny
Pianist
Born Moscow,
Russia 1971
Pages 31, 32-3

Kleiber, Carlos
Conductor
Born Berlin,
Germany 1930
Page 11

Knussen, Oliver (l)
Composer
Born Glasgow, UK 1952
Page 46-7

Kovacevich, Stephen
Pianist
Born Los Angeles,
USA 1940
Page 87

Kremer, Gidon
Violinist
Born Riga, Latvia 1947
Page 97

Kubelik, Rafael
Conductor
Born Býchory,
Slovakia 1914
Page 110

Kurtág, György
Composer
Born Lugoj,
Romania 1926
Page 66

Levine, James
Conductor
Born Cincinnati,
USA 1943
Pages 140-1

Ligeti, György
Composer
Born Discöszentmárton,
Romania 1923
Page 71

Lott, Dame Felicity
Soprano
Born Cheltenham,
UK 1947
Page 135

Ludwig, Christa
Mezzo-soprano
Born Berlin,
Germany 1928
Page 166

Lupu, Radu
Pianist
Born Galati,
Romania 1945
Pages 23, 174-5

Lutoslawski, Witold
Composer
Born Warsaw,
Poland 1913
Died 1994
Pages 80-1

Ma, YoYo
Cellist
Born Paris, France 1955
Page 122-3

Maazel, Lorin
Conductor
Born Neuilly,
France 1930
Pages 202-3

Mackerras, Sir Charles
Conductor
Born Schenectady,
USA 1925
Page 147

Marriner, Sir Neville
Conductor
Born Lincoln, UK 1924
Page 153

Masur, Kurt
Conductor
Born Brieg,
Germany 1927
Page 194

Maxwell Davies, Sir Peter
Composer
Born Salford, UK 1934
Page 79

Mehta, Zubin
Conductor
Born Bombay,
India 1936
Page 115

Menuhin, Lord (Yehudi)
Violinist
Born New York,
USA 1916
Died 1999
Pages 94

Messiaen, Olivier
Composer
Born Avignon,
France 1908
Died 1992
Page 69

Milstein, Nathan
Violinist
Born Odessa,
Ukraine 1904
Died 1992
Page 96

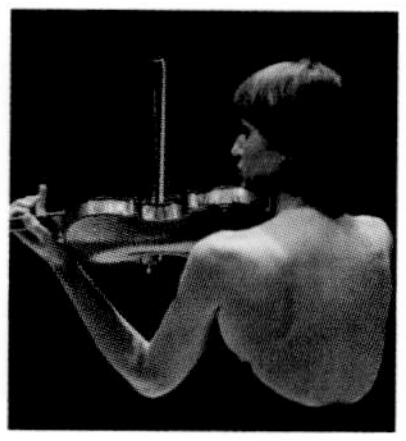

Mullova, Viktoria
Violinist
Born Moscow,
Russia 1959
Pages 102-3

Munrow, David
Early music specialist
Born Birmingham,
UK 1942
Died 1976
Page 183

Mutter, Anne-Sophie
Violinist
Born Rheinfeldin,
Germany 1963
Page 38

Norman, Jessye
Soprano
Born Augusta,
USA 1945
Pages 172-3

Norrington, Sir Roger
Conductor
Born Oxford, UK 1934
Page 152

Ogdon, John
Pianist
Born Mansfield
Woodhouse, UK 1937
Died 1989
Pages 82-3

Oistrakh, Igor
Violinist
Born Odessa,
Ukraine 1931
Pages 98-9

Ormandy, Eugene
Conductor
Born Budapest,
Hungary 1899
Died 1985
Page 113

Otter, Anne Sofie von
Mezzo-soprano
Born Stockholm,
Sweden 1955
Page 13

Ozawa, Seiji
Conductor
Born Hoten, China 1935
Page 193

Pappano, Antonio
Conductor
Born London, UK 1960
Page 60

Pärt, Arvo
Composer
Born Paide,
Estonia 1935
Page 76-7

Pavarotti, Luciano
Tenor
Born Modena,
Italy 1935
Pages 158-9, 206-7

Pears, Sir Peter
Tenor
Born Farnham, UK 1910
Died 1986
Page 178

Perahia, Murray
Pianist
Born New York,
USA 1947
Pages 84-5, 174-5

Perlman, Itzhak
Violinist
Born Tel Aviv,
Israel 1945
Page 16-17

Pollini, Maurizio
Pianist
Born Milan, Italy 1942
Page 89

Popp, Lucia
Soprano
Born Bratislava,
Slovakia 1939
Died 1993
Page 42

Previn, André
Conductor
Born Berlin,
Germany 1929
Page 204

Price, Leontyne
Soprano
Born Laurel, USA 1927
Page 170

Rampal, Jean-Pierre
Flautist
Born Marseilles,
France 1922
Died 2000
Page 182

Rattle, Sir Simon
Conductor
Born Liverpool,
UK 1955
Front cover

Richter, Sviatoslav
Pianist
Born Zhitomar,
Ukraine 1915
Died 1997
Pages 176-7

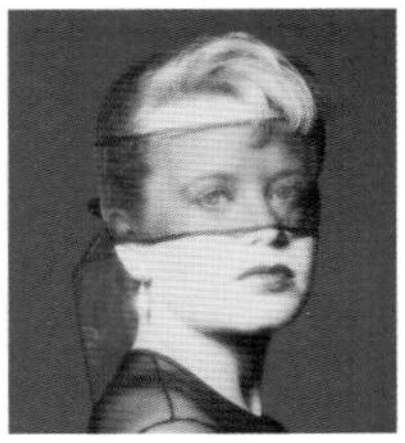

Roocroft, Amanda
Soprano
Born Coppull, UK 1966
Page 45

Rostropovich, Mstislav
Cellist and conductor
Born Baku,
Azerbaijan 1927
Pages 35, 209

Rubinstein, Artur
Pianist
Born Lódz, Poland 1887
Died 1982
Pages 50-1

Salonen, Esa-Pekka
Conductor
Born Helsinki,
Finland 1958
Pages 190-1

Sanderling, Kurt
Conductor
Born Arys,
Germany 1912
Page 187

Schiff, András
Pianist
Born Budapest,
Hungary 1953
Page 88

Scotto, Renata
Soprano
Born Savona, Italy 1933
Pages 141, 164

Serkin, Peter (r)
Pianist
Born New York,
USA 1947
Page 46-7

Serkin, Rudolf
Pianist
Born Eger, Austria 1903
Died 1991
Page 34

Shafran, Daniil
Cellist
Born St Petersburg,
Russia 1923
Died 1997
Page 36

Shankar, Ravi
Sitar player
Born Varanasi,
India 1920
Page 52

Shostakovich, Maxim
Conductor
Born St Petersburg,
Russia 1938
Pages 108-9

Sinopoli, Giuseppe
Conductor
Born Venice, Italy 1946
Page 201

Slatkin, Leonard
Conductor
Born Los Angeles,
USA 1944
Page 198

Solti, Sir Georg
Conductor
Born Budapest,
Hungary 1912
Died 1997
Page 155

Sondheim, Stephen
Composer
Born New York,
USA 1930
Page 78

Stern, Isaac
Violinist
Born Kremenets,
Ukraine 1920
Page 104

Stockhausen, Karlheinz
Composer
Born Burg Mödrath,
Germany 1928
Page 67

Stokowski, Leopold
Conductor
Born London, UK 1882
Died 1977
Page 112

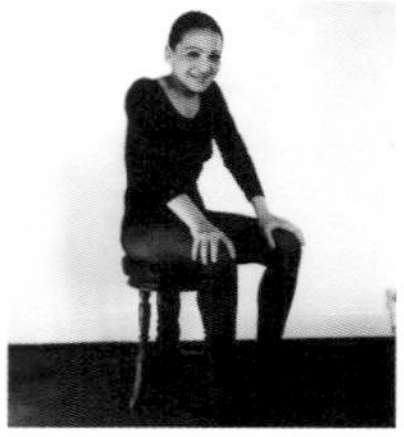

Stratas, Teresa
Soprano
Born Toronto,
Canada 1938
Page 44

Sutherland, Dame Joan
Soprano
Born Sydney,
Australia 1926
Pages 137, 206-7

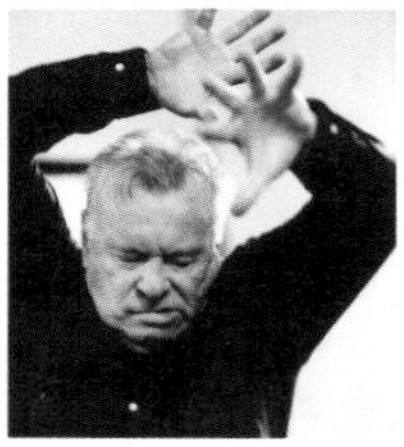

Svetlanov, Evgeny
Conductor
Born Moscow,
Russia 1928
Page 192

Takemitsu, Toru
Composer
Born Tokyo, Japan 1930
Died 1996
Page 72

Tate, Jeffrey
Conductor
Born Salisbury, UK 1943
Page 146

Temirkanov, Yuri
Conductor
Born Nalchik,
Russia 1938
Page 111

Tennstedt, Klaus
Conductor
Born Merseburg,
Germany 1926
Died 1998
Page 10

Tertis, Lionel
Viola player
Born West Hartlepool,
UK 1876
Died 1975
Page 126

Thielemann, Christian
Conductor
Born Berlin,
Germany 1959
Pages 196-7

Thomas, Michael Tilson
Conductor
Born Hollywood,
USA 1944
Page 200

Tomlinson, John
Bass Baritone
Born Oswaldtwistle,
UK 1946
Page 168-9

Tortelier, Paul
Cellist
Born Paris, France 1914
Died 1990
Page 125

Tortelier, Yan Pascal
Conductor
Born Paris, France 1947
Page 124

Troyanos, Tatiana (l)
Mezzo-soprano
Born New York,
USA 1938
Died 1993
Page 164

Tuckwell, Barry
French horn player
Born Melbourne,
Australia 1931
Page 180-1

Turnage, Mark-Anthony
Composer
Born Grays, UK 1960
Page 73

Uchida, Mitsuko
Pianist
Born Tokyo, Japan 1948
Page 90-1

Wand, Günter
Conductor
Born Elberfeld,
Germany 1912
Page 186

Williams, John
Guitarist
Born Melbourne,
Australia 1942
Page 53

Zehetmair, Thomas
Violinist
Born Salzburg,
Austria 1961
Page 105

Zimmermann, Tabea
Viola player
Born Lahr,
Germany 1966
Page 119, 120-1

Zukerman, Pinchas
Violinist and conductor
Born Tel Aviv,
Israel 1948
Page 16-17

Clive Barda: self portrait
Royal Opera House
London, 23 October 2000